For Your Garden

BIRD AND
BUTTERFLY GARDENS

For Your Garden

BIRD AND BUTTERFLY GARDENS

WARREN SCHULTZ

FRIEDMAN/FAIRFAX
PUBLISHERS

A FRIEDMAN/FAIRFAX BOOK

© 1996 by Michael Friedman Publishing Group, Inc.

Library of Congress Cataloging-in-Publication Data available upon request.

ISBN 1-56799-266-8

Editor: Susan Lauzau
Art Directors: Jeff Batzli and Lynne Yeamans
Designer: Andrea Karman
Photography Editor: Colleen Branigan
Production Associate: Camille Lee

Color separations by Fine Arts Repro House Co., Ltd.
Printed in China by Leefung-Asco Printers Ltd.

For bulk purchases and special sales, please contact:
Friedman/Fairfax Publishers
Attention: Sales Department
15 West 26th Street
New York, New York 10010
212/685-6610   FAX 212/685-1307

Table of Contents

INTRODUCTION

A flash of color catches your eye. A sweet note sounds from a corner of the garden. The landscape feels alive.

Birds and butterflies breathe life into any garden. They're flying flowers, adding the dimensions of motion and sound to the scene. The garden that attracts birds and butterflies is constantly changing and full of surprises. We stop and stand in anticipation of their visits, treasuring the moment they arrive.

We consider ourselves fortunate when birds and butterflies visit our gardens, but their appearance doesn't have to be an infrequent stroke of luck. Just as surely as we plan for vegetables and blooms in season, we can arrange for the regular appearance of wildlife.

It's amazing how little it takes to lure these creatures. Part of the planning involves undoing old garden practices. In the drive for tidy, orderly gardens confined to island beds in a sea of lawn, we've made our landscapes uninviting to birds and butterflies. All our mowing, clipping, and spraying has made our gardens aseptic and lifeless.

Fortunately for us, and for the birds and butterflies, we've begun to see the beauty of natural gardens: wildflower gardens and designs that recreate the feel of meadows and prairies make wildlife feel right at home. But you don't have to build a nature preserve in your backyard. It doesn't take much—the right flower, tree, or shrub—to lure those wild and wonderful creatures. Provide water and shelter, and you will soon find that the air is alive with color and sound.

ABOVE: Birds bring unpredictability to the garden, providing color combinations that flowers can't. You'd be hard-pressed to find a bloom that matches the electric blue of this western jay. Even if you could, who would think of combining it with the deep pink of the rubrifolia rose?

OPPOSITE: You may find yourself blessed with a crowd. On a still, sunny day, clouds of butterflies may descend on favorite plants, such as these purple coneflowers.

ABOVE: A birdbath can serve as a centerpiece for a formal garden. It's a utilitarian piece that also serves to create a mood. The gardener can count on an aerial parade of birds making the trip from the birdbath to the birdhouse hanging in the tree.

LEFT: A birdbath can be as unobtrusive as this stone bird trough, nestled at the base of black-eyed Susans. Here, it entreats birds to come and bathe, and its rustic look is perfectly in keeping with this natural garden.

OPPOSITE: Time seems to stand still as a hummingbird visits. The faint buzzing of the wings and the darting flight mesmerize both children and adults. Red tubular blossoms, like those of this delicate cardinal flower, are a welcoming beacon to these magical little birds.

ABOVE: Of course, we're all eager for the sight of the first robin. A good cover of trees will provide shelter and nesting sites for this harbinger of spring. And here's one bird who appreciates an area of lawn for good insect and worm hunting.

OPPOSITE: Ranging from Pennsylvania to Florida to Texas, the zebra swallowtail is a butterfly unlike any other. Its triangular, black-striped wings and graceful tail make it easy to identify as it stops to feed on the nectar of flowering trees and vines.

ABOVE: Butterflies bring harmony to the garden. In flight and even at rest, butterflies offer gentle curves and graceful movement, softening the divide between flora and fauna. Here, the wings of a great speckled fritillary mirror the curve of purple coneflower petals.

OPPOSITE: The eastern bluebird is making a comeback, thanks entirely to dedicated backyard birders who erect houses for the pest-eating, social birds.

ABOVE: Some of the best garden designs devote wide expanses to a single hue. A moment of contrast heightens the effect of otherwise undiluted color. These coneflowers never look more white than when visited by a bright peacock butterfly.

OPPOSITE: Butterflies weave a unique texture into the garden. A silky butterfly poised on a spiky thistle adds an unexpected contrast. Its translucent wings make the most of early-morning and late-afternoon light.

LEFT: Fruit trees in the garden attract many birds, including the rose-breasted grosbeak. They often descend in huge flocks, filling the air with their liquid, mellifluous song. Welcome them, and they'll return the favor, feasting on harmful insects.

RIGHT: The rewards of taking the time to plan and maintain a backyard bird habitat are many. You may get the rare chance to watch a red-winged blackbird grow into an adult.

ABOVE: A male cardinal is a welcome visitor year-round. He's a fine enough sight in spring when the garden breaks into bloom, but the flash of red is even more uplifting in winter when all else is drab. A good planting of seed-producing plants, supplemented by a bird feeder, will convince the cardinal to stay.

Chapter One

PLANNING THE BIRD AND BUTTERFLY GARDEN

Birds and butterflies are accidental tourists in virtually any garden. As long as there is something growing and flowering, an occasional winged creature will pass through. But with a little planning and planting, you can increase those numbers and ensure that birds and butterflies return regularly.

There are scores of flowers and trees that can be planted to attract birds and butterflies, and if you're really serious you can make your landscape irresistible to them. At the same time, you'll be creating an environment that's just as pleasing to you and your family.

As with any garden, planning is most important. An understanding of wildlife habits is required, but birds and butterflies are not demanding. In many cases their preferences coincide with ours.

There's nothing exotic about the requirements of these winged visitors: trees and vines for shelter, perching, and nesting; open sunny spaces; blocks of colorful flowers to provide nectar and seed; selected plants to provide food for larvae; a reliable source of water. How you fill in the blanks is up to you.

In many ways, planning for birds and butterflies makes gardening more straightforward. It provides a goal and a structure for your energies, and as your design takes shape, you're sure to find it seducing you as well.

OPPOSITE: Bright, single-colored flowers with good, strong foliage for perching tempt all types of butterflies. By planting in pots, you can situate these butterfly magnets in plain view of a window. The flowering vines on the wall also help to bring a variety of birds to the area.

BELOW: Birds and butterflies have a few basic needs in the garden. They're not that different from ours: food, shelter, and security. Birds need a place to perch, preferably with protective cover nearby. This restful area does double duty in the wildlife garden: the verbena spilling over the bench and the coneflowers in the background also attract butterflies.

ABOVE: A few nasturtium seeds sown in the spring can provide quick cover and transform a landscape. The bright yellow and orange flowers are favorites of both hummingbirds and butterflies (although Fido seems unimpressed).

OPPOSITE: Both birds and butterflies are enticed by broad, sunlit areas. Butterflies like to bask in the sun while feeding. And flowers grown in the sun produce the most nectar.

RIGHT: Don't be in a hurry to pick up the ax or chain saw to clear away dead trees. They often contain treasure troves of insects that woodpeckers will gladly hunt for.

BELOW: A mixed planting provides the best odds of attracting many different species of birds and butterflies. However, butterflies are attracted to clusters of same-colored flowers, such as the mass of orange blooms in this cottage garden. A progressive garden, with plants maturing and setting seeds at different times throughout the year, also increases your chance of success.

OPPOSITE: During winter, a feeder full of sunflower seeds will keep blue jays coming back. A stand of trees in the landscape provides perching spots and shelter throughout the year.

ABOVE: Where do butterflies come from? From caterpillars, of course. All butterfly larvae have specific food preferences, such as these sawfly larvae that are feeding on a prunus leaf. The best butterfly habitats have larval host plants as well as nectar producers.

LEFT: You can't go wrong if you think natural in the garden. And nothing is more natural than a meadow or prairie. In such a planting there is plenty to lure wildlife, and little to discourage them: no mowing and no pesticides. The trees in the background provide ideal perching and nesting areas.

OPPOSITE: Evergreen trees and shrubs provide shelter for birds, such as this white-crowned sparrow, throughout the year. Many also produce small "nuts" that make excellent food for over-wintering birds.

RIGHT: If there are two features that are important in the garden, they are cover and color. This dense bush provides plenty of protection for the natural, flowering feeding stations below. Give thought to the landscape as a whole. Your long-range plan should include shrubs for perching, nesting, and protection, with bright color splashed throughout. And don't forget to consider your vista from the house.

Chapter Two

BUILDING FOR BIRDS AND BUTTERFLIES

A well-designed mix of plants will attract birds and butterflies. Other garden features will convince them to return and maybe even set up house. These little creatures have needs beyond plants for food and nectar. They need places to perch and roost, to lay eggs, and to overwinter. They need water and protection from the elements.

Birdhouses, bird feeders, and birdbaths can transform a garden into a sanctuary. At the same time, they add a decorative element to any garden. They offer the opportunity for creativity beyond arrangements of plants and flowers and provide visual interest when the flowers are out of season.

Birds and butterflies also flock to areas where the hand of man is not so evident. They're attracted to dead trees, crumbling stone walls, and unmowed meadows. Fortunately for us, these features in themselves enhance the look of the landscape.

OPPOSITE: A simple picket fence can frame a garden bed beautifully. This one mirrors the upright habit of the flowers. At the same time, it's a perfect place to find birds perching during the day.

LEFT: This tumbled-down wall adds a sense of history to the landscape. While serving as a perfect backdrop for plants, it creates a friendly habitat for birds and butterflies, and provides good shelter and nesting areas. It's also a fertile feeding ground for birds, who can hunt among the stones for insects.

ABOVE: A birdhouse can be a charming addition to any land-scape. The charm wears thin, however, if the birdhouse is ignored by the birds. It pays to know the housing requirements of the birds you want to attract. Chickadees, for example, prefer a house about six to fifteen feet (1.8 to 4.5m) off the ground. Ideally, their house should be in or near a tree, but in shade that is not too deep.

OPPOSITE: Imagine the delight of sighting birds swooping out from their home in a rose bower. The simple style of this birdhouse doesn't compete with the lush beauty of the flowers. The rose vines provide cover to protect the inhabitants, and many roses bear hips that provide food for birds.

RIGHT: Birdhouses provide the opportunity for whimsy in the garden, becoming design elements themselves. Many birdhouses are built to be seen, and some birds, such as wrens, bluebirds, and purple martins, are drawn to houses erected in the open.

RIGHT: Some birds are sociable creatures that enjoy "apartment" living. Though most birds are ruled by territoriality and will nest only in solitary boxes, swallows and purple martins prefer the company of others. This behavior provides the opportunity for elaborate birdhouses such as this one.

ABOVE: The rustic nature of these birdhouses emphasizes the natural feel of this corner of a damp, shady garden. By echoing the texture of untreated wood, even a simple stump looks like a garden accent, and wild creatures appreciate the untamed surroundings.

RIGHT: Both birds and butterflies are drawn to water in the garden. The simplest way to provide it is with birdbaths. They can add ornamental interest in both formal and informal gardens and provide a focal point around which to group plants.

OPPOSITE: A water garden can transform a landscape while providing a place for birds to bathe and drink and for butterflies to refresh themselves. The addition of plants increases the attraction, and the water garden becomes a habitat for snails, slugs, and insects that provide food for birds.

ABOVE: Planting in pots allows you to combine attractive features in the garden. The verbena and other flowering plants in this pond-side container act as a beacon for butterflies.

ABOVE: A rock wall is virtually a bed and breakfast for butterflies and birds. The nooks, crannies, and crevices in this wall offer natural shelter and food for birds as well as nesting sites for overwintering butterflies. The trailing flowers offer their nectar for butterfly residents and visitors alike.

OPPOSITE: You can attract scores of birds with the proper plantings, structure, and water. But for some birds, only seed will do for food. A ceramic or wooden feeder can add an elegant touch to the landscape. A combination of feeders allows you to offer a number of different types of seed to attract different birds. Thistle will draw goldfinches, for example, and sunflower seeds appeal to evening grosbeaks, chickadees, cardinals, and other birds.

ABOVE: A bird feeder need not be elaborate. A simple feeding tray, with a roof to keep off the elements, will do. This finely crafted roof adds an element of class. Make sure to place the feeder in view of a window or deck so you can fully enjoy the visiting birds.

RIGHT: A bird feeder in the right place can convert a corner of the landscape into a special place. This unremarkable lattice fence is transformed by the thatched-roof feeder.

OPPOSITE: Japanese honeysuckle is a favorite of hummingbirds and butterflies. This trellis not only shows the riot of fragrant flowers to advantage but supplies a perching place as well.

OPPOSITE: The monkey flowers spilling over an old log make an intriguing planting. The cracks and crevices in the log provide good hunting for birds, and after a rain, water pools in the hollows, providing refreshment for birds and butterflies. This quirky arrangement is right at home in a natural or wildflower garden.

ABOVE: Butterflies need to soak up sunlight to maintain the high body temperature that allows them to stay active. A simple flat stone in the sunshine provides a perfect solar refueling site. Mottled stone is a good choice because it provides camouflage protection for some butterflies.

Chapter Three

BLOOMS FOR BIRDS AND BUTTERFLIES

*F*lowering plants are the stars of any landscape, but they are especially important in the bird and butterfly garden. That, of course, is what flowers are all about: attracting birds, butterflies, and bees as pollinators.

There are scores of flowers that will attract butterflies, so you will have lots of design options. Bright, tubular blooms are a signature of the plants that butterflies most often prefer. Many other plants have foliage that serves as food for larvae and as sites for egg-laying. Still others produce seeds favored by birds.

Some of the most popular perennials fit perfectly in the specialized garden. But you don't have to wait years for a bird and butterfly planting to mature and begin attracting those lovely flying creatures. There are many quick-growing, early-flowering plants that will begin working their magic almost as soon as they hit the ground. Whether your garden is large or small, you're certain to find plants that not only lure birds and butterflies but suit your tastes as well.

OPPOSITE: Introducing color into the garden is a snap with snapdragons. Bring them home from the garden center in the spring and plop them in the ground for an instant riot of color. It won't be long before the buckeye butterfly finds them.

RIGHT: Asters are easy to grow and are native throughout much of the United States. In the autumn, the New England countryside takes on a bluish hue as they burst into bloom. Asters add a casual, cottage-garden look and are a favorite of the pearl crescent butterfly, which uses them as a larval host plant.

ABOVE: Most farmers and many gardeners are not big fans of milkweed, but the monarch butterfly literally cannot live without it. The flowers provide nectar for the adults, while the foliage serves as an egg-laying site and provides food for the larvae.

OPPOSITE: You can grow your own bird food (with built-in bird feeder) if you plant sunflowers. Make a patch at the rear of your flower bed or vegetable garden and let the seeds mature. Birds will flock to feast on them. The plant also plays host to the patch butterfly in the Southwest.

ABOVE: The butterfly bush has been called catnip for butterflies. Many species, including the huge mourning cloak, the bright orange comma butterfly, and the classic tiger swallowtail, seek it out for its nectar.

LEFT: Yarrow is a long-blooming perennial that ensures clusters of colorful blooms throughout the summer. Its diminutive flowers act as a beacon for the American painted lady butterfly.

OPPOSITE: Not traditionally regarded as a butterfly-attracting plant, delicate bleeding heart flowers are attractive to a few species, including the red-spotted white butterfly *Clodius parnassiun* in the Northwest. These flowers are a good way to add color to a shady corner of your wildlife garden.

ABOVE: Even if you have a wet, marshy area, you can plant butterfly-attracting plants, such as this native boneset plant. A member of the aster family, boneset has long been a favorite for its easy cultivation and its clusters of grayish white to purple flowers.

OPPOSITE: This boisterous planting shouts color all summer long, and both birds and butterflies respond to its colorful call. The latter are drawn to the golden gaillardia, while hummingbirds can often be found sipping nectar from petunias. This blazing shade of pink is one of the colors most attractive to them.

ABOVE LEFT: The herb garden can be a friendly place for wildlife. These blocks of color beckon to butterflies, who feed on the allium plant in the foreground. The salvia in the rear attracts hummingbirds.

ABOVE RIGHT: Tickseed, or coreopsis, is a must for the meadow or wildlife garden. Its nectar draws butterflies, such as this red admiral, while the seed heads are favored by birds, including goldfinches and sparrows.

OPPOSITE: Petunias are such a common annual, especially in formal beds and gardens, that they're often overlooked in the wildlife garden. They can't be beat for long-lasting color in the ground or in pots and window boxes, and they are a reliable hummingbird favorite.

ABOVE: Johnny-jump-ups show their bright faces in the spring, providing an early-season source of nectar for many butterflies. The plants self-sow and naturalize rapidly. Plant a few, and you'll have plenty in following years.

OPPOSITE: Daisies are a favorite of many species of butterflies, including the fiery skipper, queen, and red admiral. As an added bonus, daisies bloom from late spring to early autumn, providing season-long color in the garden.

ABOVE: Impatiens are one of the most popular bedding plants because they bring an instant shot of bright color to a shady area. And they're as popular with hummingbirds and butterflies as they are with gardeners. Plant them in a shady bed, or even better, fill a window box to overflowing so you'll be sure to have a good vantage point for viewing the creatures that visit.

OPPOSITE: Elecampane is a weedy, rough-leaved plant that blooms freely from July through September and is often found growing wild along roadsides. There, and in the natural garden, it will attract a wide selection of butterflies, who feed on the nectar.

LEFT: The purple coneflower is a native perennial that looks equally at home in formal garden beds or in cottage gardens and meadows. Wherever you plant it, butterflies, including the painted lady, are sure to gather.

RIGHT: Lavender is vital to any herb garden or meadow planting. It's common to see butterflies fluttering through the sweet-smelling flowers.

OPPOSITE: Contrast in the garden is visually pleasing and allows you to satisfy most winged visitors with plants that suit their varying needs. Here, yarrow draws butterflies all through the summer, while the round seed heads of the eryngium are attractive to birds.

ABOVE: Many thistle flowers serve as nectar sources for butterflies and hummingbirds. Later in the season, the seeds serve as food for birds such as goldfinches.

LEFT: A good bird and butterfly planting provides food and shelter all through the growing season, with nectar-producing flowers blooming in sequence from early spring to autumn. Goldenrod, with its late blooms, keeps butterflies coming back well into the end of autumn.

OPPOSITE: The intriguing, bell-shaped blooms of the foxglove are also attractive to hummingbirds. You'll often find them zooming from bloom to bloom, enjoying the nectar. The plants make a bold statement in the early summer garden when they're grouped in a mass, either in full sun or dappled shade.

Chapter Four

THE FRAMEWORK OF THE BIRD AND BUTTERFLY GARDEN

he backbone of a wildlife garden is the permanent planting that provides cover, protection, and nesting and breeding sites, as well as food and nectar. All through the year, no matter what the climate, there are plenty of trees and shrubs you can plant to attract wildlife.

Trees and shrubs offer the opportunity to turn your landscape into a haven for birds. Berries, fruits, and nuts produced throughout the year will entice birds; evergreens provide shelter during autumn and winter; and flowering vines supply nectar, as well as cover, for these small creatures. You'll delight in the sight of a single jay swooping down from a majestic maple tree or a flock of chickadees bursting from the cover of an arborvitae. You'll take comfort in knowing that you're planting for the future, providing a sanctuary that will last long after the last flower has bloomed.

OPPOSITE: The black locust is a stately tree for nearly any landscape. Native to the eastern United States from Pennsylvania southward, even a single tree can be picturesque. It produces white flowers, followed by a fruit pod. The fruit is attractive to bobwhites and mourning doves.

ABOVE: The brown thrasher is a garden virtuoso. Its song is loud, clear, and musical; and like the better-known mockingbird, it possesses the gift of mimicry. It's well worth planning a planting to lure this sweet singer, which enjoys wild strawberries and the fruits of the dogwood.

OPPOSITE: Any kind of vine will offer a haven for birds and butterflies. A combination of wisteria and clematis makes a thicket that they can nest in safely. Its many species, with their wide variety of growth habits and flower forms, make clematis a versatile climber; wisteria is a garden classic, though it often takes several years to bloom. These flowering vines put the finishing touch on any garden, even as they welcome winged creatures.

ABOVE: Diversity is the key when designing the skeleton of the garden. Start with a tree that's a crowd pleaser among the winged and feathered crowd and build around it. Birch trees are good choices, as they produce a small nutlet that is favored by a number of birds, including juncos, blue jays, goldfinches, titmice, and even pheasants and great blue herons. It's also a host for the beautifully mottled clouded locust underwing butterfly.

ABOVE: Lucky is the gardener who hears the tap-tap-tapping of the pileated woodpecker hunting for food in a tree. The sight of this huge, red-crested bird is enough to make a backyard birder's day. It nests in a hole excavated in a dead tree or shrub, so you may elect to leave some deadwood on your property to draw this eye-catching bird.

RIGHT: Fruit trees are one of the most valuable elements in the bird and butterfly garden. Many species of fruit trees are small enough to fit into even a modest backyard, and they mature early, providing fruit for birds. Nectar-loaded blossoms court butterflies and hummingbirds, and birds can usually count on finding a variety of insects to snack on. Here, the fruit trees are combined with a cutting-flower understory.

ABOVE: A tangle of wild grasses and buttercups beneath a tree offers the best of both worlds to birds, who find protection among the leaves and food among the grasses.

OPPOSITE: The tiny downy woodpecker is an omnivore that will gladly feast on the fruit of mulberry or wild cherry. In winter months, when fruit and insects are scarce, you can lure it to your garden with a suet feeder.

RIGHT: You don't have to wait for the holidays to deck the landscape with boughs of holly. This beautiful plant grows as either a shrub or a tree, and some species are hardy throughout most of North America. The bright red berries are considered a treat by many birds, including woodpeckers, mockingbirds, flickers, and bobwhites.

ABOVE: Birds are opportunistic, and sometimes surprisingly creative, when it comes to finding a nesting site. A mass of foliage hanging in a sheltered spot seems like the perfect place for a robin's nest. Who cares if it turns out to be a hanging plant on a porch?

OPPOSITE: When well trellised and pruned, a berry patch can be an attractive part of the garden. In fact, raspberries and loganberries are related to the rose, the wineberry being one of the more attractive of the genus. You'll find the fruit quite sweet if you can beat the birds to it.

ABOVE: Blueberries are a must for any edible landscape. They're such a favorite of wildlife that birds are considered the main pest in commercial plantings. The attractive plants burst into delicate, white, bell-shaped flowers in the spring. The fruit is followed by bright red foliage in the autumn.

ABOVE: Planting fast-growing flowering vines near an outdoor seating area creates a pleasant bower where you can observe the wildlife up close. This glorious mass of fragrant honeysuckle is certain to draw a myriad of birds and butterflies.

ABOVE: A healthy, vibrant landscape maintained without toxic pesticides provides plenty of food for young bird families.

RIGHT: In the spring, horsechestnut trees are covered with blossoms. The trumpetlike flowers are a favorite nectar source for hummingbirds.

BELOW: Trees are vital for creating a year-round bird habitat. They provide shelter and support for overwintering birds, such as this chickadee, when all else in the garden is dead or dormant. Regular attention to a feeder or two can keep birds coming back all winter long.